WORLDLY VIEWS

ONE WOMAN'S COLLECTION OF TRUE SHORT
STORIES FROM AROUND THE GLOBE

ANGELA MACKAY

Copyright © 2025 by Angela Mackay

All rights reserved.

No part of this book may be reproduced, stored in a retrieval system, or transmitted in any form or by any means—electronic, mechanical, photocopying, recording, or otherwise—without the prior written permission of the author, except in the case of brief quotations used in reviews or critical articles.

This is a work of nonfiction. The events and stories described in this book are based on real occurrences and the author's personal experiences. However, names, places, and identifying details may have been changed to protect the privacy of individuals.

Any resemblance to actual persons, living or dead, beyond those identified in the text is purely coincidental.

Published by Striking Content Inc.

Print ISBN: 978-1-069-1701-1-8

The author is not responsible for any actions taken based on the content of this book.

THIS BOOK IS DEDICATED TO

My companion travellers.

Sometimes, we left for our travels together with a map, a plan and a schedule. Other times, it was far more chaotic or coincidental.

Many travellers I met by chance en route and we shared various journeys to monuments, mountains, deserts, oceans, palaces, and one time, a pigsty! We had adventures and made discoveries, both about ourselves and the places we explored. Some became friends and we remain in touch, while others drifted along distant paths.

Such is the nature, the passion and the joy of travel.

I remain hopeful of meeting many more along the way.

– A.M.

CONTENTS

Foreword	vii
1. Selena The Pig	1
2. Dinner In Carmona	10
3. Ephraim	18
4. Bandit Country	23
5. Into Albania	28
6. The Gin Palace	33
7. D'ye Ken John Rae?	40
8. The Italian Chapel	46
9. Dushanbe, Buzkashi And The River Of Gold	50
10. Looking For Adam	57
11. No Trains Today	65

FOREWORD

My original collection was titled "Short Stories for YOU." It was a humble treasury intended exclusively for my children and grandchildren to give them a sense of my history. I wanted them to know "what grandma was up to all those working years." On a deeper level, it was my intent to introduce my family's youngest generation to the vastness of the world and all the possibilities that come along with it.

This original writing quest evolved into eleven stories from nine different countries. Scotland, which I very recently discovered with such delight, gets two contributions because this is my heritage and I believe everyone ought to know where they come from and what that information means in the grand scheme of their lives.

I must tell you, the stories you're about to read are not typical travel tales. They're not situated in tourist-heavy holiday hot spots or particularly famous locations. Some take place in an area of the world I briefly visited, while others reflect a location of long-term

FOREWORD

residence. Through all of my unique experiences, I was rarely alone entirely and rather was often in the company of strangers or work colleagues, and occasionally, "old friends."

In these pages, you will travel from the Orkneys to the streets of Addis Ababa and the mountains of Tajikistan. There will be dining in Angola with an archbishop, and encounters with both a monstrous pig and an armed bandit!

The sentiment of the conclusion to the final story speaks best to the magic of travel:

"...the best part is never knowing who you're about to meet on the next plane, or train or bird observatory. And perhaps even better, you never know what brilliantly unexpected conversations you may find yourself in as you explore those human connections that serve as a genuine grounding on this enormous and amazing home, Planet Earth."

These words are courtesy of Katie Kuperman of Striking Content, who I can never thank enough for helping me launch this worldly collection of short stories, and for being such a wonderful editor, guide and colleague along the journey.

I hope you enjoy!

- - Angela

SELENA THE PIG

*S*elena was a large, lonely sow. She led a solitary existence at the Shashe school farm, with a lack of available males to suit her. Even for a pig she was unlovely.

From 1970 to 1972, I was a teacher at Shashe River School, situated in Tonota, Botswana. Attached to this high school were four 'brigades' for non-academic students – somewhat akin to vocational training in carpentry, building, textiles and farming. Shashe was funded primarily by external donors and was, to some extent, regarded as an experiment by both the donors and the Botswana Ministry of Education. Needless to say, it was always short on cash.

Our deep sympathies for Selena's spinsterish existence as well as our consideration for the potential revenue from the sale of her progeny, gave rise to a cunning plan.

Charles was the instigator, regaling us with eye-rolling histrionics of Selena's loneliness. But finding a mate was no easy task. Pigs were few and far between in Botswana. It took weeks and required that local pig owners, of whom there were very few, be contacted to source a suitor with specific qualifications. Bulk, poor vision and passion were top priorities.

At last, a candidate was found. Volunteers were summoned to take the school truck and bring the lucky boar back to Selena's pen. Given the fact that we were on-call volunteers much of the time and were accustomed to volunteering for all kinds of things, no-one thought to praise our public-spiritedness or question our sanity.

The day arrived, dawning dull and wet. It was that time of year which would be autumn in any temperate climate. But here, no specific name can be given to the short, unpredictable time that is not even a season, but more of a frame of mind in tropical regions. The days were hot and the nights cool, with cold, drizzly days emerging unexpectedly when least needed.

Such was the day of the "Great Pig Expedition." When we left school, it had been raining for some hours and the tracks were a mess. The other volunteers and I were anything but happy, huddled in the back of the Bedford truck. It wasn't heavy rain – more of a soaker than a gusher, piddling non-stop, determinedly saturating every layer of our clothing, with puddles sloshing on the truck bed. The stretching horizons and the still, sun-drowned beauty of the scrub appeared as a bedraggled lunarscape, deserted and depressing.

True to form, our driver, Mudongo, stopped twice – once to fill his front seats with a group of wet but laughing women and the second time to fill the back with a woebegone family of countless kids and mothers. Clustered together behind the cab for the minimal warmth and shelter it provided, we were not a cheerful bunch. And Mudongo did not make life any easier. Careering at full tilt through pothole and mud alike, he sent us slithering across the back seats as he crashed his brakes or attacked quagmires with verve rather than skill, emerging stern first. Irritable yells to slow down were met with casual, smiling waves from his window but no change to his driving.

After multiple queries, wrong turns and endless miles of identical, character-less tracks, we arrived at a large wooden stockade. It was time to meet the groom. Once introductions and greetings with the pig-owner's family were complete, we were led to a row of small, smelly, inter-connecting pens of wooden stakes. With much snorting and hefty prods to his grubby rump, the beast was persuaded to appear. Not a pretty sight. If Selena was no porcine Venus this specimen was far from Adonis.

He was not especially large, but thick-set and stubby with broad shoulders into which sunk a short, pointed head. His colour was of dark greyish black, unlike the virginal lightness of Selena's downy flanks. He smelt abominable, and snorted loudly and frequently. The most arresting feature was its face, or rather its snout, crowned with a pair of the longest, curliest, most evil-looking tusks one could imagine. Poor Selena.

After the initial viewing, it didn't take us long to realize that pig transportation was one thing but how were we to coax the boar onto the truck? First impressions told us he was no friendly character and had likely never left his home farm. This was not going to be easy, particularly for the likes of us – a clueless group without the slightest experience handling large pigs!

First, he needed to be named – and then tamed. Beastie came naturally as a name. Taming was another story. There was speculation that it would be easier to bring Selena to visit – but there were obligations to the farmer that the pig would leave with us.

Leaning on the stockade, we gambled on our chances of survival while the farmer's family watched from a distance, no doubt amused by the spectacle of ill-equipped pig handlers, awaiting the circus that would result.

Much daunted but feigning knowhow, Mudongo agreed to bring the truck into the compound, find a spot among the ditches where he could park with the back wheels lower than the front, and then lower the tailgate to form a ramp for Beastie.

Armed with a long rope we set out for the pen. Beastie's living quarters did not improve his temper. The stockade was barely eighteen inches longer than the animal and just wide enough to allow turning space or room to squeeze through a hole into the adjacent pen. An array of equally ugly pigs lived in the six interconnecting pens constantly snorting, squealing, honking and bumping as they skittered from one pen to the next, dodging Beastie the King.

First task: block the holes on either side of the pen to prevent Beastie's escape and the entry of his nosey neighbours. This was accomplished by one of the braver farmhands who clambered along the stockade, clutching and swinging from overhanging branches to keep balance, as he thrust stakes into the ground.

Beastie, already disturbed by the onlookers and the blocked exits, began to make charges at the stockade. Chunks of wood dislodged by his tusks fell to the ground like bananas sliced with an axe. Mudongo came to offer unsolicited advice and performed a vivid mime of what was likely to happen to us if Beastie got loose. The future was bleak. With that, Mudongo disappeared to the driving cab and there was one remaining general agreement among us: if Beastie got loose, climbing the thorn trees was the only available, yet unattractive, option for survival.

Beastie pawed the sand.

Our master plan was about to begin. We made a noose in the rope and dangled it temptingly in front of Beastie's head while he was gently prodded from the rear. In a perfect world, he would move forward into the noose that proceeded to be tightened and together we would swing our considerable weight on the end of the rope to keep a grip on him. When he stopped rushing around trying to escape, we would push and drag him up the ramp, tie him down and be off. Simple.

But Beastie had other ideas.

At first, he slumped down under his shelter and had to be prodded into the upright. His mood deteriorated. The farmhands teetered on the stockade dangling the noose while Beastie assumed a range of awkward and disobliging stances, within flicking distance of where we wanted him.

Patiently the boys prodded, murmured to him and shifted the noose until Beastie was perfectly lined up with it directly in front of him. Robert and Nick were poised ready to whip out the stakes so he could be squeezed out of the pen once the noose had caught.

It was a breathless moment – would he or would he not? His shifty little eyes darted from side to side, he lowered those evil tusks as he sniffed the rope and to our amazement, slid his head neatly into the noose. For a moment nothing happened. Then the boys tightened the noose. Beastie stood there, uncomplaining and obliging. Once he was securely caught, the stakes were pulled out, leaving a hole big enough for him to squeeze through.

Or so we thought.

We were wary but also lulled by his quietness and our false sense of belief that the job was virtually finished.

In an enormous jerk of the rope, several hundredweight of angry, hairy pig launched through the opening and rushed, snorting into freedom.

The rope slipped from the farm boys' hands as they tried vainly to clutch it, before tumbling to a heap in the pen. Robert and Nick leapt for the stockade, the farmer's family disappeared, the other pigs set up a great squealing and snorting while the rest of us took off, as predicted, in every direction that did not contain a mad boar.

Helpless with laughter, Mudongo watched from the safety of his cab.

Beastie charged and snorted, then stopped, snorted some more and stamped the ground. He rammed his head at an imaginary adversary, turned round and charged off in another direction. He stopped, pacing and snorting, not only angry but mystified by his newfound freedom.

Slowly, cautiously, we emerged from hiding, keeping low to the ground in best tracking practice, trying to fool Beastie that he was not being approached by a bunch of half-wits. Fortunately, he wasn't interested in us, more bemused by the space around him.

The men closed in. Dave yelled at Anne and I to keep out because "the men" would handle it. We did not argue.

To our surprise they succeeded. Gingerly picking up the dragging end of the rope, four of them closed in on the animal. They tugged hard, brought Beastie to his knees and began dragging him along the ground. Upon hearing the wretched noise he kicked up, it was tempting to feel sympathy for the ranting beast. We would be sure not to tell Selena of his humiliation.

The farm boys came to help while Beastie made his muddy way to the truck, roaring, snorting and gnashing his tusks. Getting up the ramp was even more difficult. Someone had to be brave enough to touch the creature and push it from behind as others pulled from the front. The farm boys and Nick prodded with their hands and pushed with sticks while Anne and I made our important contribution from the truck side rails, exhorting everyone to "heave!" Mudongo, uncomfortable at the closeness of the animal in his precious truck, hung out of his window offering detailed Setswana instruction on how to tie Beastie securely.

One way or another the trussed beast was lashed to the deck, tight enough to be secure, but loose enough to move around at a safe distance from its captors. We lined the sides of the Bedford, hanging onto the rails and crossbars, muscles taut and ready to clamber up and off if Beastie made one false move. Mudongo needed no second bidding to head for home.

Our prisoner was restless. He huffed and snorted, kicked out his leg and tried to stand, only to slide to failure on the slipperiness of the deck. Tugging at the ropes, Beastie strained his shoulders against the bonds and continually bashed his snout on the floor in frustration.

There was no sympathy. The tracks were washed out with enormous deep puddles and patches of viscous mud caught at the wheels, swinging us maliciously off course. Mudongo was urged to go faster and, not wanting to be near the beast longer than absolutely necessary, he obliged. The return trip became an endurance test as we clutched the rails and were flung around the slippery deck, the whole time feeling anxious, not wanting to get caught up in the restraining ropes and keeping a cautious eye out for the angry pig.

At one point, with a gargantuan heave, Beastie struggled onto three feet and lunged at Nick who disappeared feet first over the side of the truck. We stopped, the ropes were tightened, Nick climbed back on board and for the rest of the journey there wasn't a relaxed muscle among us.

The return to school was hardly triumphant. The rain had driven everyone indoors and we quickly headed for the farm where Selena waited. Backing up to her pen and sliding and pushing the creature out was a piece of cake. He landed with a crash, angry, confused and possibly as tired as we were. Selena stood unmoving in the corner, closely observing her suitor.

There was no love at first sight (understandable) and no quivering leap to greet him, which might be expected of a potential mate. Perhaps her sheltered life had not prepared her for hasty recognition of the opposite sex. Beastie scowled and flicked his nasty little eyes around his new surroundings, letting them linger not a moment too long on his bride. He snuffled and snorted, and then stood silently brooding. We decided to retreat, allowing them privacy. It seemed indelicate to watch their shy advances.

I wish this tale had a happier ending.

Beastie certainly qualified with regard to bulk. His eyesight was questionable, but most importantly, passion was clearly lacking.

It appears that pigs cannot be persuaded to squander their emotions when their hearts are not truly captured. Hilarious predictions were made about the earth tremors we'd hear when these two beasts consummated their affections. The first night we all slept in peace, knowing them for cautious creatures that would not engage in a whirlwind romance.

Sadly, all our nights were undisturbed by tremors or piggy howls of ecstasy. Charles, keeping a watchful eye on the pair, crept up to the pen on many a night, hoping to observe a couple intoxicated by love, but reported only disappointment.

It was a stand-off. They stood as if transfixed, staring at each other from their respective corners, or wallowing deep in separate slumbers. Interested viewers would visit the pair during the days to whisper encouragement, but to no avail. It was not shyness that kept them apart. Beastie would snuffle and honk away in his fashion while Selena looked at him with eyes filled with porcine disdain. She did not like him. And who could blame her? He was an ugly, smelly, uncouth lout. And Beastie, for all his vicious behaviour with his captors, never seemed to think of forcing his attentions on so delicately-hued and genteel a lady porker.

We were disappointed after all our efforts that Selena was not to be a happy mum and that there would be no piglet income for the school. After a couple of months Beastie was returned to his home and Selena was alone once more. Only temporarily, that is, until her fate was sealed as sustenance, having outlived her other potential purposes.

Farming is an unsentimental occupation, and not long after this adventure, we were eating more sausages and bacon than any of us care to remember.

DINNER IN CARMONA

More than 40 years later, the contents of the dinner are forgettable but the company and the context remain as clear as events of yesterday, unlikely ever to be forgotten.

The dinner took place in Carmona, now called Uige, Angola in 1976. Angola had recently become independent, following the signing of the Alvor Agreement in 1975 by the three previously warring parties, the MPLA, FNLA and Unita. Portugal, the former colonial power, withdrew its troops and November 1975 saw the official declaration of the Independence of the People's Republic of Angola. This was interpreted as a victory for the Marxist MPLA, led by Agostinho Neto, with its primary power base situated in the centre of Angola, Luanda.

Holden Roberto's Frente Nacional de Libertação de Angola (FNLA) was a fading force. It retained American support, however, not because Roberto was a particularly effective leader, but because the US supported him as a bulwark against Russian or Cuban influence, and secondarily, as an ally of President Mobutu in Zaire (later renamed as Democratic of the Congo (DRC) in 1997). It was believed that Roberto received an annual salary from the US government in return for local intelligence. He was also promoted as a descendant of the royal family of the Bakongo people, which lent him something of a cachet and increased his potential value to supporters.

Jonas Savimbi's group, União Nacional para a Independência Total de Angola (UNITA), was supported by the largest ethnic group in the country, the Ovimbundu. Located mainly in the south, UNITA later emerged as a major spoiler during continuing years of civil war, with support from apartheid South Africa.

In 1976, Angola was more or less calm with occasional outbursts of militia enthusiasm dotting the countryside, feeding a tension and insecurity that flavored our journey.

Sadly, civil war soon erupted and continued for years. After the end of direct colonial rule by Portugal, the remaining conflict was a blend of the politics of a riven society divided on ethnic and urban/rural spectrums, and the massive interference of foreign military and political involvement. It was a Cold War proxy: Russia and Cuba supporting the MPLA, and the United States funding the FNLA.

For a time, the country remained uneasily divided in three; the fighting had subsided and a tenuous peace was declared. It did *not* make for comfortable travel.

At the time, we were working for Oxfam, a non-governmental humanitarian organization whose purpose was to assess the needs of people returning home from Zaire after years of displacement. This evaluation was required to determine whether or not there was a need for Oxfam's assistance through a cross-border relief operation.

We were based in Kinshasa, Zaire. It was here where we met Père de Munck, a Belgian priest who considered the people and territory of both the Bas Zaire Province and Northern Angola to be his parishioners and his responsibility. Quite impressed by him, we agreed to join the priest on an assessment mission.

We left for Angola via Bas Zaire, the most southerly province of Zaire. For de Munck there were no borders, only his extensive parish in a diocese that lapped over formal frontiers. His primary concern was to identify the most urgent needs of his parishioners as they returned to the homes they had long abandoned. With first-hand knowledge from conversations with the people and by visiting the lands upon which they planned to settle, make fertile and farm, the priest would be able to make effective appeals to the catholic authorities and other international aid agencies for support. Père de Munck, known and trusted by the people and conversant in their language, was a ready source for the information required by Oxfam. Off we went!

The returning population, ethnic BaKongo, had lived in related communities for years in Zaire and would need to survive planting and growing seasons before returning to a chance of survival on their own land. We trusted de Munck, his notions of a borderless land and his skills of navigation, as we threaded the Land Rover through the northern provinces. Our battered Michelin map was left behind. It was my first lesson in the political value and danger of lines on maps. I was never quite sure when we crossed from Zaire into Angola.

Travelling from the north, the countryside was pastoral, mainly tranquil green, rolling hills that inspired a sense of normality. The silence, however, was not normal. Only ruins remained. Farmsteads had rotted and crumbled, heaps of mud and sticks littering the landscape; and the cattle were dead, slaughtered long ago. The coffee plantations that had been the foundation of the local economy were abandoned and the bushes had run amok.

Driving along poorly-maintained roads, severely pot-holed, gouged and washed out in the rainy season, we followed behind the trickle of people returning, coming mostly from their refuge in the BaKongo communities of Bas Zaire Province. They had little baggage but the tiges (stems) of manioc they hoped to plant when they reached home. Manioc has limited value as food except to provide bulk and a sense of fullness. It grows like a weed – simply stick it in the ground and it sprouts, needing little skill or attention to cultivate.

The haphazard roadblocks on the deeply-rutted roads were controlled by teenagers waving machine guns and clutching rosaries. Their attire was an assortment of camouflage pants and t-shirts adorned with the icons and imagery of the wealthier places that donated them.

A few ruined buildings were all that remained of a thriving district centre. Graffiti slogans for the FNLA smeared the walls of the health post, proclaiming victory. The stone buildings had collapsed and been engulfed by creeping vegetation. My eyes locked on a giant elephant skull perched on a crumbling wall, its empty eye sockets gazing reproachfully on the world below. Like the livestock, it was a victim of starving people. All the wildlife and birds had been hunted. It was a silent place.

At one point we passed a police post, with a view from its porch over the soft green of the coffee plantations in the valley. It reeked of shit and dead vermin. The armed group of young militias occupying the post gladly posed for photos – both with and without sunglasses. Without, their smiling gazes were intense and mildly disturbing.

Throughout our journey, we stayed overnight at remote missions, run by monks from Portugal and Italy - Franciscans and Capuchins - clinging to the routines that had sustained them for centuries. It was a grudging hospitality.

At the first of the missions, in their threadbare monkish garb, using only candles for lighting, skinny monks with sad faces were visibly rattled by a female presence. My husband and I were banished to separate cell-like rooms as far apart as the building permitted. At a meagre but wholesome meal with wine, the brothers talked with de Munck about their work in the communities that were slowly rebuilding.

After the initial fulsome greetings in assorted languages, the brothers and the Père assumed an efficient and professional demeanor. His questions to the fellow religious practitioners were serious, as he searched and inquired repeatedly for more information. He listened intently, never a written note taken, as he bent towards them to hear every answer, frowning and questioning again and again. Lacking either Portuguese or Italian, it was a challenge to follow, but French and Latin were my friends and I grasped the bare bones.

The monk's claim was that the mission's purpose was to provide education and health services. I don't doubt that this was its intention, but my skepticism took over. This was not pure. The goal of missionary work, to maintain and expand the numbers and commitment of the faithful was to me, a misdirected and dishonest sub-text to their worthy practical activities. de Munck seemed at home with the brothers but I suspected, belying his bonhomie, he shared some of the same skepticism. For all his faith, he was an intensely practical man, more concerned at that moment with the survival of the returnees than their spiritual needs, which he would attend to in time.

Another night was spent at an abandoned mission building that housed yet more of de Munck's congregation. The floor of a former school-room was covered in beans from the coffee harvest spread out to dry. There were hopes of selling it once transport was available. The young boys talked of buying food and new shirts. In a corner of the same room, a young woman was conducting lessons for a group of children without texts, notebooks or pencils. She wrote with sticks of charcoal on the rough white walls.

De Munck's remaining store of food that he maintained in the building was less than promising – cans of oily sardines and wormy rice. Not appetizing in the slightest, but it would have been churlish to object.

On the third day of travel, we reached Carmona. This was the provincial capital of the northern renamed Province of Uige, the heartland of the former BaKongo Kingdom and major coffee producer. It had little aspect as a bustling city and rather felt abandoned and empty. We were lodged, thanks to de Munck's request, at the Archbishop's Palace. After the simplicity of the mission life we had briefly shared, this was surprisingly spacious, a place of marble and polished wood, grand staircases and statues, walls covered in religious paintings – and electricity. Instead of the celibate cells of the missions, my husband and I were granted a huge double bed and a marble bathroom – with hot water.

Underdressed for such splendour, but clean, unlike de Munck still in his grubby soutane with dribblings, we were called to the dining room. An indoor fountain and mini waterfall tinkled over marble stones at the far end of the room. A large dining table filled its centre.

We were a motley crew: myself, a Brit, my husband, a Canadian, Belgian lay nurses, a Polish doctor, a mysterious American, Swiss Red Cross workers, and priests from Portugal. What a babel of voices we were. His Excellency, the Archbishop and the most fluent of us all, began a conversation about the federal-provincial political interplay in Quebec in perfect French; he joked with the Swiss in German about their gnomic qualities as guardians of wealth; reverted to more hesitant Flemish with the nurses and de Munck; and shared uproarious jokes in Portuguese with his fellow religious members. He switched back and forth from one language to another as freely and as often as various parts of the multi-course meal arrived at our table, served by a small army of Angolan retainers.

The mysterious American, rumoured to be a close companion of Holden Roberto, was not ignored. He was questioned, with little subtlety and in perfect English, about the ease of purchasing fuel and other supplies in the north of the country. His sullen response, *"What we need we take",* brought temporary silence and a passing frown to the genial Archbishop.

Under the watchful eye of the second-in-command, handsome Monsignor from São Tomé, we ate from bone-china and drank Portuguese wine from crystal while swapping war stories.

Liqueur and coffee were served in the adjoining lounge where the Archbishop, ever charming and erudite, continued chatting with each of us in our native tongue. He also played the glossy grand piano, accompanied by the Monsignor who sang liquid, heart-rending Portuguese love songs, his affectionate gaze on the pianist never faltering.

Outside on the pock-marked buildings, the littering of political graffiti scrawled by a generation of liberation warriors was invisible in the enveloping darkness. Inside, a fascinating group of individuals, each unique in their own right, who otherwise never would have crossed paths, spent an odd yet beautiful evening together.

Sometimes life has a curious way of designing the most unlikely and unforgettable experiences that remain forever.

EPHRAIM

*H*is full name was Ephraim Abraham Selassie. Although we never found out his precise age, he appeared to be in his early twenties. Out of nowhere he burst into our lives, stayed a few minutes and then was gone.

My son, 17 at the time, and I were driving home in rush hour traffic with the most blinding sun slant piercing through our windshield when we heard a voice call out to us.

"Madam, which way to airport?"

I replied with as brief and straightforward directions as possible. It wasn't easy approaching Abiot Square with a major intersection of six roads and it also wasn't easy to be clear which was the "right" road. He set off running like a man possessed.

As we crossed the square minutes later, we saw him again, still running with his arms pumping, fast and determined. There he was, in the middle of the square, dodging lines of traffic, making his choice of exit. The wrong one.

Foiling the taxis, we called out, told him it was the wrong road and gave terse explanations of how to get to the airport road.

"How long running to airport? One hour, two?"

"No, half an hour."

"Which way airport? Jimma Road?

"No, you're going the wrong way for Jimma Road. Where do you want? Bole Airport or Jimma Road?"

His face collapsed and tears trickled down his cheeks.

"Oh no. Oh please Madam, I'm sorry," and he wiped his eyes and his fingers. "No, sorry, but I just get free, out of jail. I must get to Jimma Road, old airport. I am going home."

His distress affected us both. I'll never forget what my son said next.

"Mom, we have to help him!"

I told the man to get in the car. There was something very compelling about this earnest, tearful man who ran with such passion.

He kissed my arm that was lying on the window frame.

"Oh, thank you, thank you."

He asked us for nothing, but gave everything through his story. Now that his running had been given a reprieve, all that focused energy tumbled into the words he used to tell his tale.

He had been in jail for two months short of 15 years. His father, Abraham Gebre Selassie, a senior member of the Ministry of Defence under the Emperor Haile Selassie, had been shot when the Marxist Dergue (the name given to the government in Ethiopia from 1974-1987) came to power in 1974. As strong as the rays of the sun that day, we could sense the great pride Ephraim had for his late father. After this death, Ephraim was imprisoned, later taken from jail to serve in Mengistu's army in 1986. Since the fall of the Dergue in 1991, he'd been in prison in Assab, Eritrea.

Two days before we met him, he was set free. Determined to get to Ulubabor, one of Ethiopia's most westerly provinces, he hitched rides on long distance trucks to Addis. Now, he was running.

In the "Mercato" where the buses left for destinations all over the country, he was chased and stoned as a thief by suspicious residents who didn't know what to make of a penniless man trying to hitch a free ride home.

Originally, he'd asked us for directions to Jimma Road – "the road to home." Yet we found out that "home" was 700km from Addis, where we were now.

We asked how he would get there.

"Running. I running all way."

Why was he running; what was there?

"Mamma. Very much love."

I knew my son and I both shared the same thought. After 15 years, how did he know his beloved Mamma was still alive?

He asked where we were from. When I told him Canada, he squeaked his delight and flung his arms around the back of my car seat.

"Canada. Oh, I have sister in Toronto. She escape."

He took my card with my Ottawa address from the centre console of my car, and left us his name, which he wrote on a scrap piece of paper. As we found Jimma Road, I checked with a cab driver that the military hospital, a landmark Ephraim had been told to look out for, was nearby.

He told us how frightened he had been of hyenas at night during his journey to Addis, and how it would take him another three days to get home, running and hitching rides, but it would only take three *hours* by plane.

He wept again, his hand to his eyes. "I free now, fifteen years in jail – now I free."

We left him just below the military hospital. I reached my hand out with some money for him – it wasn't enough for bus fare, but I didn't have any more cash. At the least it would get him some food and maybe a bed away from the hyenas. He kissed my son, who hugged him in return, and promised to write to Canada to let us know he had arrived home safely.

The last we saw of Ephraim were his hands waving and blowing us kisses as we turned out of the parking lot.

My son burst into tears. A big, strong seventeen-year-old boy, crying at the injustice of the world that keeps another boy in jail for his youth, far away from his home and without the love of his family. And I wept with him at this cursed loss of Ephraim's innocence in a world often unfit for his goodness. But I also wept for another reason. I wept with intense pride for my son and his beautiful instincts that day. I felt extremely fortunate to have had him with me for the full 17 years of his life – a number just in excess of Ephraim's jail term.

It was October 11, 1994 and I had been stationed briefly in Addis Ababa working for the Ethiopian Relief and Rehabilitation Commission, "on loan" from CARE Canada. My son, always exploratory, had asked to come with me for the school term so he could experience Ethiopia and "have adventures." Oh, adventures we had, let me tell you. We explored whenever possible, and my son had the best academic term of his school career at Sandford Secondary School.

When we returned to home base after our encounter with Ephraim, we were eager to tell our Ethiopian friends the story. A little to our surprise, they were skeptical of Ephraim's tale. Sadly, the culture of suspicion and secrecy, nurtured by the Mengistu years, dehumanized the best of people. Such stories abound. Every family was somehow touched by excesses, obsessions, arbitrary cruelty and persecution by the Dergue. Ephraim was not alone, and yet on that day, I suppose it wasn't time for others to see him deserving of particular sympathy.

I checked myself repeatedly – the rational mind sought explanation, testing the reflexes of the emotional self. I reflected on our encounter, ashamed to doubt, but needing reassurance. Why did I need evidence that I wasn't gullible, rather than proof that I was human?

I do not doubt he was genuine, his story true. It was the way he ran, single-minded and passionate. It was the way he wept and the flutter of his hands as he said goodbye. Besides, he had absolutely nothing to gain by telling me lies. All we offered was a short, free ride and a handful of miserable coinage.

That night I thought of Ephraim as I listened to the collective midnight barking of the neighbourhood dogs and the rustle of the cool night wind in the eucalyptus. I prayed he was safely on his way. Not given to prayer, what passes for a plea in the silence of thought was perhaps the best I could manage.

I hoped he succeeded. Because he deserved it. Because life is unjust and unfair, and for the thousands like him, it would be good for the scales to tip a little in their favour. Because it would feel good to know we helped a little. Because I wanted so much for my own son's faith to stay intact. And most of all, because it would mean that a boy made it home to another mother who loved her son.

BANDIT COUNTRY

A cracking sound came from the thorn scrub to my left. My hope was that it was a very large camel stepping on a very dry branch – at the most, careless gun-cleaning or the product of an anxious imagination.

Ironically, just one night before in the gallows humour of people who work in tough conditions, I had laughed with others as they competed to tell the funniest and most outrageous hijacking tale.

Now it was happening to me.

I found myself on the road between Dadaab Regional Support Centre for Somali refugee camps and Hagadera, a camp of some 40,000 souls in Kenya's northeast province. It was 1995 and I was working for a Canadian NGO that managed basic services for more than 200,000 refugees on behalf of the UNHCR.

I suppose you could call four well-armed Somalis stepping onto the road ahead, delivering several more gunshots into the air, sufficient enough evidence to convince me that this was, in fact, a hijacking in the works. It was obvious that Patrick, the driver and camp supervisor at Hagadera, was tempted to floor it and take a couple of bandits on the hood. Sense prevailed, however, and he stopped in a slither of sand and dust. Sprawled in the back of the cruiser with me was Eddie, the camp manager who sent a distress call over his handheld radio just in time.

One of the bandits toted a homemade RPG (rocket-propelled grenade) on his shoulder. These guys were serious. Calmly, Eddie talked us all out of the vehicle, as the bandits surrounded it, waving weaponry. Empty hands resolutely held high, we walked slowly away from the vehicle and towards the bush. They fired shots at Patrick's feet, demanding the car keys. He shook like a jelly and barely gripped the keys as he handed them over. As he slipped from my peripheral vision a thought occurred that I was abandoning him, not knowing if he was hit. There was nothing I could do.

They proceeded to take our radios. I lost sight of the other four men I was with. For a brief period, I feared they would shoot us all, and if they didn't, I'd be walking into the bush forever. There was no end in sight. My logical mind insisted they only wanted the vehicles and would leave passengers free in the bush. My terrified mind interrupted, recognizing that in this situation, anything could happen. If they were high on ghat (a plant also known as miraa, related to marijuana, whose leaves are chewed for their stimulating effects) they might not know or care what they did. They could be angry, vengeful, careless...there were no rules of engagement here.

I continued walking forward, praying that the shot meant for me would come from behind. I didn't want to see it coming. I thought about how awful it would be for my children to hear the news and fleetingly saw my bloodied body lying in the red sand, numb to the scratch and tug of pernicious thorn bushes.

One of the bandits followed me, yelling in Somali, gesturing for me to throw my sunglasses to him. I did, turned and continued walking.

Then the fellow with the RPG came, waving the damn thing around in the air as he also gestured at me. I became acutely aware that I was the only female in the group. Up here, as victims of inter-clan feuding, women were often raped when they went to collect firewood or tend to their herds. Once again, rational thought competed with fear. I am white, a non-Muslim, unclean, untouchable. I hoped. But when was rape ever anything but an act of anger and humiliation? I hoped the others wouldn't risk their own lives trying to protect me.

The bandit wanted my $25 watch and a silver bracelet. Thank God, or Allah, or whoever. A small price to see his departing back.

On the road behind me, I started to hear what could only be described as a lack of driving skills. With the engine revving madly, the driver wrestled with the deep, loose sand that grabbed and stalled the tires as he turned the vehicle.

Then just like that, they were gone, racing back the way we had come.

Several minutes later, I finally laid eyes on the others. Intent on staying invisible from the road, we walked deeper into the bush and headed for Hagadera. A moment later the police, alerted by Eddie's distress call, roared up the road in pursuit of the bandits. Anxious to avoid any crossfire we flattened ourselves on the ground behind the thickest thorn trees.

A loud and convincing gunfight followed, and then – shots close by. With a single mind we all feared the bandits had returned to take us as hostages. Somehow, with the outside temperature still in the upper 30s Celsius, in deep sand, snagged by every avenging thorn tree, we ran. Oh, we ran.

The shots faded and so did the danger. We passed bundles of abandoned firewood and footprints disappearing into the bush. We tracked fresh tire prints which convinced Patrick that this was organized crime and the bandits had been driven to the attack site.

Banditry is endemic in Kenya's northeast province even still to this day. The vast sand and thorn scrub, crossed by few vehicle tracks, dotted with wells, occasional settlements and nomadic herds are features that make the environment ideal for acts of robbery by armed groups. Home to the 'Shifta Wars' of the then-Northern Frontier District under colonial dispensation, whether afflicted with marauding cattle rustlers or feuding tribes, it has long been known as 'shifta' country. Today it is Somalis who raid over the porous border, stealing vehicles for competing clan faction leaders. The roofs are sliced off, machine-guns mounted and another 'technical' is born to continue warfare by other means.

Half an hour later, dirty, sweaty and very thirsty, we cautiously emerged at the edge of Hagadera camp. We were going to live! Empty oil drums and a Land Rover barricaded the road. There, walking towards me was Dahabo, a giant of a woman and Somali social worker who I'd met before.

"My God, is it you? Are you well? We were so worried about you all," she said, as she enveloped me in her armfuls of perfumed robes and hugged me close. I said nothing, but welcomed the warm hug with great relief after what had been the most frightening experience of my life.

Not but a moment later, a parade of police vehicles came searching for us, looking very smug and satisfied. They had rescued the vehicle and its contents but announced that the bandits had escaped on foot. The Kenyan military were tracking them.

The initial distress call had alerted everyone – as it's meant to. Hand-held radios are "de rigueur" for all aid agency staff so our adventure had been broadcast far and wide – plus the fact that the police had lost us.

The vehicle in question, parked behind the road barricade was rapidly becoming a thrilling play space for a swarm of small boys. Time to move fast. Shooing them out of the way not a minute too soon, I reached under the back bench seat. Held my breath. Yes, there it was, stuffed under the seat before anyone noticed, my small pack with all the essentials – money, passport…and my camera. Wouldn't those small boys have enjoyed that treasure!

We returned to Dadaab in a convoy of aid workers, labourers and military, noisy and relieved. As we set out, the heavens opened and the deep, rutted tracks instantly turned into a quagmire. The rain smiled down on the bandits, whose tracks were washed away drop by drop.

The unmistakable sweet smell of African earth after a big rain accompanied us back to Dadaab, which sat reassuringly at the end of an emerging rainbow up ahead.

INTO ALBANIA

It all happened because a single shepherd pursued his sheep without an ounce of respect for legal borders.

There he was. The shepherd was sent back from Albania to Kosovo, scooting down the hillside and home across the border, hands tied behind his back, holding a grenade. Minus the sheep.

The German United Nations Civilian Police (UNCIVPOL) responsible for the area in Kosovo relieved him of the grenade, promising to go in pursuit of his stolen sheep. At that time, the UNCIVPOL had executive authority in Kosovo while the reformed Kosovo Police Service was under development.

NATO, known as Kosovo Force (KFOR), didn't have a mandate in Albania. The Rambouillet Agreement in June 1999 authorized 30,000 peacekeeping troops into Kosovo, which was later supported by the Security Council Resolution 1244. The mission was known as UNMIK. KFOR was the military presence, while the civilian presence was led by the UN. This included UNHCR (in the beginning), OSCE and the EU. Other UN agencies were present as well, but these shifted over time. While the training of a new, reformed police service was taking place under the OSCE, in the meantime, international police were recruited to join the UNCIVPOL.

Then there was little ol' me on that day, sitting in a convoy accompanied by NATO forces, at the Morinë border between Kosovo and Albania. I seriously wondered why I was there. This had absolutely nothing to do with me. I was devoid of any knowledge about sheep and policing. My bashful presence could only be explained by the fact that I had decided to visit my Canadian friend for the weekend. Following the war, we were both civilians recruited and paid by the Canadian government to be contributors to the role of the Organization for Security and Co-operation in Europe (OSCE). My friend, Elena, worked in the small Dragas office monitoring human rights and promoting democratic practices.

All of a sudden, a shepherd ran down a hill attached to a grenade!

For reasons never entirely clear, but probably for moral support, the German UNCIVPOL officer invited Elena to go along on the mission. It seemed I was about to do the same.

The shepherd was from Dragas, an unusual community of Slavic Muslims nestled in the hills of the foot of Kosovo, wedged between Albania on one side and now North Macedonia on the other.

There was a distinct lack of formality about crossing the border. There was no Albania passport entry stamp to treasure, nor a foreign exchange and we were without leks (currency of Albania).

The countryside was unremarkable, uniformly bleak and watery under incessant rain and grey skies, that is, except for the mushrooms – the bunkers built during Albania's Communist era of the 1970s to defend the population against envisaged attack from a host of supposed enemies. They littered the land and beaches, built at crossroads, on hillsides, in gardens and throughout orchards, each resembling the flat cap of a mushroom.

Sheep grazed on every hillside. How could shepherds identify the sheep out here? They all looked exactly the same. So did the shepherds.

Our shepherd was warmly ensconced in the UN police car, affectionately known as "Coca-Cola cars", for their red and white stripe.

Then, with no warning, we were driving off the road, through a field, into the mud, then even more mud – and far away. This was pursuit. Had the German UNCIVPOL officer miraculously spotted the shepherd's flock? Are those distant fuzzy blobs the lost sheep of Dragas?

Seemingly not. After much muddy manoeuvring and clods of flying earth surrounding us on all sides, we were back on the dreary road.

There were no more sightings, only the endless drizzle, forlorn homesteads...and sheep. Outside the Town of Kukës, the lurid green dribbles of factory effluent on the banks of the River Drin provided a combination of brilliant colour and an appalling reminder of the careless pollution of ex-President Hoxha's industrial dreams.

Following our arrival in Kukës, the Albanian Police Commandant was notified of the convoy's entrance and proceedings became even more surreal.

It was a Sunday morning, and therefore, a day off for the Commandant. He entered, clearly displeased, accompanied by an ever-expanding retinue of underlings. We were ushered into a large conference room where the Commandant assumed the chair behind a bank of phones (the way it was before cell phones) and proceeded to lift one receiver, shout, bang it down and shift to the next one. Every time one of the phones rang, he seized the receiver, listened briefly, barked orders and slammed it back down.

This seemed unlikely to end well.

The young male underlings in their sharp Italian suits and even sharper haircuts scurried briskly, stepping obediently in and out of the room, constantly gathering more instruction and dashing about. The room filled. Who were all these people?

I sat on the rim of the room, hoping to be invisible as the drama unfolded before my eyes. The display of phone power subsided and the reason for the visit of German UNCIVPOL officers was explained. Our NATO convoy waited outside – after all, they were only there for security reasons, but the Commandant made a clear point he was most unhappy with NATO sitting on his doorstep.

Suitable outrage was expressed that a Kosovo shepherd should be robbed of his sheep and it was admitted that there were, indeed, many criminal sheep-robbers in the countryside. Perhaps the shepherd could speak for himself and describe his experience. Translation was, in fact, available.

But the shepherd was outside, locked in the police car. He didn't trust the Albanian police and no inducements could persuade him to come out.

The German policewoman was asked to give her evidence of the condition of the shepherd, the grenade and everything else pertaining to the situation. Was she really rummaging in a shoebox for her notes? Afraid so. No wonder the need for moral support.

The Commandant was not impressed but it was Sunday morning and no more time could afford to be wasted. The coming and going of the smart young men continued, the phones rang and the receivers were continually picked up, bellowed into and banged down. But the Commandant smiled, re-affirmed the commitment of the Albanian police to pursue the criminals and return our Kosovo shepherd's sheep. I figured they were surely mutton stew by now.

He declared that NATO could go home, thanked UNCIVPOL for their diligence and proceeded to enjoy a celebratory coffee.

As I sit here some 20 years later, it's quite tempting to wonder how bored the police officers were that day, or how much they wanted to be seen as "active" by the local community. After all, Albania was a very nasty place under the regime of Enver Hoxha, which explains, at least to some extent, the dilapidation and chaotic nature of the police services.

Interestingly enough, it's my impression that UNCIVPOL had no legal authority in Albania. They did, however, make some effort to communicate and collaborate with the Albanian police over the border at times, which explains their actions to help the shepherd find his sheep – it wasn't downright outrageous, just a bit cheeky, I suppose.

As the entourage crossed the street to a café, I was instantly reminded of our lack of leks. How would we pay? The crystal-clear vision of an Albanian police cell loomed again. Luckily the beaming Commandant was happy to host the three "lovely ladies" and I refused to cringe at the term or deny my loveliness. We smiled with thanks.

The shepherd remained outside, locked in the UN police car. Still, there wasn't a chance he was going to put his trust in the Albanian police.

THE GIN PALACE

Flying to Barentu was a surprise gift. Barentu, west of Asmara, was situated in the fertile country somewhat close to the Eritrean border with Sudan. The Gin Palace was an even greater surprise.

I was curious. The accounts of a colleague who had worked with the humanitarian Operation Lifeline, and who had great admiration for Isaias Afewerki (the first and only President of Eritrea since 1993), combined with my reading of Thomas Keneally's *"Towards Asmara"* long whetted my appetite.

Eritrea had a tumultuous century since becoming a colony of Italy in 1890. This land, believed to be part of ancient Punt – God's Land – with pieces of what are now Somalia, Ethiopia and Sudan, was occupied in 1941 by British forces that ousted the Italians. In 1962, annexation as a province of Ethiopia led to 30 years of war, prior to independence in 1991. Finally, in 1993 Eritrea's independence was officially recognized – only to revert to war with Ethiopia again in 1998 because of a border dispute.

Those are the bleak historical milestones. There was also the more romantic vision of the combination of Eritrean and Italian art during the brief occupation by Britain. Then there was Assab Port, once the only entry point for supplies to Ethiopia and the new Eritrea, along with the torturous climb up the mountainside from the Red Sea to Asmara. The times were also characterized by a blend of Orthodox Christianity and Islam, the sentimental perceptions of desert people and the promise of the iridescent Red Sea waters. In other words, there was history, half-truths, misty longings, propaganda and limitless curiosity.

I had previously read an abundance of literature surrounding the work I was there to complete. In my studies, I came across several accounts by Eritrean women who had joined the liberation forces in the 90s and worked alongside men, living in shelters cut into mountains. It was very much "back to the kitchen, girls" when the war was over.

Throughout the country, there was ultimately a tenuous peace, maintained by the presence of peacekeeping forces that dotted the land. Eventually, tempers cooled and the Border Commission made final deliberations about which bit of stony ground belonged to which country.

Previously, I'd driven from Asmara through the Eritrean countryside and across that flimsy border with Ethiopia. That experience made it difficult to imagine what, beyond fierce national pride, maintained the argument today. The people spoke the same languages, clung to a subsistence lifestyle scratching the stony soil, wandered with small herds and mostly worshipped in the same faith. But there were lines of trenches dug into hillsides, men fiercely waving weapons at every turn and a palpable tension.

Barentu was different. There was a large Muslim population. It was desert country. A herd of camels greeted us outside the airport and raced the military escort into town.

I was there to deliver *"Gender and Peacekeeping"* training to a Jordanian contingent of UN peacekeepers. In 2000, the UN Security Council Resolution 1325 on *"Women, Peace and Security,"* apart from being groundbreaking, had shone a spotlight where it had long been needed: on the contributions women make to every aspect of peacekeeping. This included the easily recognizable blue hats and blue berets, military and civil police, but also civilians, and above all, the women of nations caught in conflict and struggling for peace. Member states were obliged to ensure their forces were trained and that successive peacekeeping mandates made women's voices heard and included in decision-making.

I had the unenviably wonderful task of developing the first UN training program on the topic and for several months had been visiting most of the active peacekeeping missions to test drive the content. Now it was time to share it with the Jordanians and obtain feedback.

Apart from myself as Lead Trainer, there was a female Sudanese UN staffer who acted as an Arabic translator, an Australian army captain and two other African UN resource staff members who helped with facilitation and discussion, and shared their experiences in peacekeeping operations. Military and civilian expertise, along with the presence of UN staff and multiple language skills proved to be an effective combination.

Training is what I do, it's my profession and I love it. New material is always a challenge. There are fresh concepts, various languages, disputes to traditional thinking and behaviours, and a fine line that must be walked in a way that embraces clarity, patience, good humour, respect and tenacity. Gender wins the prize for a tough topic.

The crowded classroom was stinking hot and we proceeded at a comfortable pace with a very cheery crowd. Though the room was initially set up in a formal configuration with everyone seated at long tables perpendicular to the teaching space, soon the space was in total disarray as small groups formed and began working at multiple flip charts. The arrangement was designed to let groups decide whether they wanted to work in English or Arabic.

As the morning wore on, it all became a bit of a struggle. First, there was the heat – I was dripping under a lugubrious ceiling fan. Second, there was limited space for the larger than expected crowd of Jordanian military, UN civilians and local participants who showed up. Then there was the slow pace at which I was required to teach as a result of translation challenges, accompanied by many puzzled looks and lengthy explanations. Teaching gender is rarely easy, however on the positive side, I found the Jordanian troops to be most polite. They were very interested in learning more and their questions proved it, along with their unwavering willingness to accept the challenges put in front of them. Everyone carried on gamely.

My job was to make the content both accessible and practical. At the end of the day, it was always important to remember that the content itself wasn't optional. As a UN peacekeeper, they were required to obey certain conventions, laws and mandates. Deciding that gender wasn't relevant wouldn't be a smart move for any contingent.

Suddenly it was noon. Everyone stood up and walked out. First the room was empty and then the building was empty. Within minutes I found myself completely alone. My UN colleagues had also disappeared!

Then I heard it – *adhán*, the call to Friday noon prayer. What planning genius had organized this? Here I was, alone on the street outside in Barentu, at 40 degrees Celcius in the shade. I felt abandoned.

When in doubt, walk. Camera slyly at the ready I headed for downtown, passed by the occasional curious donkey and man shrouded in white, shuffling in the shade.

A woman emerged from a roadside hut, beckoning vigorously. Why not? Shade would be welcome. She led me to the makeshift building and pointed that I should sit on a low chair inside a lean-to of blankets and sacking tied to wooden poles. A man joined her, then another. Momentary panic set in as unappealing possibilities flashed through my mind. Sense prevailed. This was not an organized crime hub, the locus of a civil war or terrorism. This was hospitality.

A little stunned, I studied them as discreetly as I could. The woman who invited me in had exquisite hair, braided in terrifyingly tight and intricate patterns, bunched at the back of her head. She had such beautiful features. The first man, of a similar age, was also good-looking and sturdy, with a lightly grey-speckled beard. The older man was seemingly toothless except for two Bugs Bunny choppers. There was much greeting. Hands on hearts, small nods and smiles.

There was no common language between us. I could only manage "yes" and "no", "please" and "thank you" in Arabic. They were thrilled.

She brought out a large bottle full of clear liquid and an unopened bottle of Sprite. She waved them around with a glass, eyebrows raised. I nodded yes. Liquid. Wonderful.

I thought water and sprite an unusual combination, but no matter, it was welcome liquid. She poured a generous glass, mixed with a hint of Sprite and I glugged it back. Gin! Oh, God. Why not? This was unexpected. A Muslim society? Gin? At midday on a

Friday? But they were not in the mosque and as she poured a small glass for each of them, it seemed not to matter.

The glass was filled again – and again – as we signalled our way through conversation with much smiling, head-shaking, hand-waving and general good manners. The old man sat on the battered sofa gazing at me longingly. This was a bit uncomfortable, until I noticed he looked at her like that too. It seemed to be his standard soulful gaze and I was merely the stranger in their midst. I was quite certain this gin sharing with a foreigner wasn't a common activity and assured myself there was nothing to fear.

The woman left the hut and returned minutes later with an enamel bowl of water and a cloth, knelt at my feet and removed my sandals. There was nothing to do but sit back and raise my glass. She soaked the sand off gently and wiped them dry, then put back my sandals and took away the basin. There was nothing I could say but "thank you" in Arabic.

I pointed at my camera and raised my eyebrows, wondering in this Muslim home. The message was received and they got organized, lined up on the old sofa. To my surprise, the quiet man put an affectionate arm around her, and the old man, moon-faced, tipped his head to one side, with an arm around them both.

It was time to go back out into the blinding sun, a little more relaxed now – or was it tipsy? We each placed our hands on our hearts and said, "Inshallah" to indicate "we shall meet again, if God wishes." With a few smiling nods and tiny waves, they were back inside the hut and I was alone again.

I walked, or perhaps wobbled, to the Jordanian headquarters for lunch. There were mountains of chicken pilaf. Etiquette required, I sat with the Commanding Officer who constantly re-piled my plate over and over again. I kept eating in the hopes that it would soak up the gin.

We were back in the classroom at 3:00p.m. I think they had an entertaining afternoon. I was floating along happily, shifting topics and timing to accommodate the shortened teaching day, but was beyond being bothered about it. There was plenty of group work for discussion as I cut and trimmed the content, searching for the essence that would at least leave a question to ponder or provoke a response. Prayer had a most agreeable effect, flexing my students' grey matter, while mine was lightly veiled in gin.

Too soon we were packing to leave. There was no flexibility as the plane was waiting and the rulebook dictated a return to Addis Ababa before nightfall. The same camels cluttered the road to the landing strip again, waiting for their next convoy duty.

As I boarded the plane and flew east into the evening hours, the gin finally subsided. I slept, with regret that no matter the influence of *"Inshallah,"* I was unlikely ever to come this way again. Yet still, I enveloped in the delight of such an unexpected day.

D'YE KEN JOHN RAE?

*I*n regular, non-Scottish English, that question means, do you know John Rae? Probably not. John Rae is hardly a household name, yet he was one of the most successful Victorian explorers, especially of Canada's north.

Around the time that my 60-something age morphed into 70, I went through a phase of exploration that delved into my ancestry. It was a moment so many of us come to at some point in our adult lives in which our focus and interest lie not solely on where we're going but also from where we've come. And of course, there was the arrival of my grandchildren to motivate my exploration of this family history I was so curious about.

Dr. John Rae happened to be one of the people I stumbled upon in my exploratory adventures and was quite captivated by his tale, and more specifically, his place in Scottish history. To add to his attraction, there was a strong connection between Scotland and Canada.

Hudson's Bay Company (HBC), was founded by Royal Charter

1670 to exploit the fur trade of Rupert's Land, around Hudson Bay. In the early 1700s, ships stopped just a little ways off from Stromness, a town located on the Orkney Islands in Scotland, to take on water from Login's Well and to recruit men to work for the HBC. By 1800, most of the employees were Orcadians, renowned for their hardiness, sobriety and boat handling. An early recruiting agent, John Rae Senior, was father of the Arctic explorer, John Rae, who contributed significantly to surveying and mapping much of Canada's northern waters. Oddly enough, John Rae is little known in Canada.

Today a statue of the explorer greets arrivals on the ferries from mainland Scotland and the islands, looking out from the Stromness pier-head towards the Hall of Clestrain, Orphir, where he was born. In his home country he is a hero, buried in St. Magnus cathedral graveyard where today a large monument of his resting figure sits inside the cathedral.

Yet his name is not found among many of the other great northern explorers such as John Franklin, Shackleton, Scott or Amundsen. His is a quieter local fame. This is the man who mapped Canada's Arctic waterways, including the discovery of the final navigable portion of the North West Passage, known as Rae Strait, between the Boothia Peninsula and King William Island. He's also the man who, according to reports from the Inuit and Cree (whose languages he knew and understood well), learned of the tragedy of Franklin's expedition boats, HMS Erebus and HMS Terror, and in 1854 reported on this knowledge to the Admiralty. It's possible that this may very well have signalled the reasons for the controversy surrounding his name beyond Orkney.

Educated at home by a tutor, the young Rae lived an outdoor life in Orphir, learning to sail, shoot, run and rock climb. From 1829 to 1833, he studied medicine at Edinburgh. Post graduation, he joined the HBC as a surgeon, spending the first winter in James Bay (he could go no further because ice blocked the Hudson Strait). Ten years with the HBC at Moose Factory followed, but the north captivated him and as there was not enough need for his medical skills, he turned increasingly to trading and exploring with the Cree and Inuit. He learned hunting skills, how to walk in snowshoes, how to build "snow houses" and to live off the land.

He was something of a man apart and was openly critical of HBC officers who landed in the north with little knowledge or sensitivity to its peoples.

"He made scathing remarks about naval officers and others who formed snap judgements after spending only a short time in the company's territories: "These self-sufficient donkeys come into this country, see the Indians sometimes miserably clad and half-starved, the causes of which they never think of enquiring into, but place it all to the credit of the Company."

(R. L. Richards, "RAE, JOHN (1813-93)," in Dictionary of Canadian Biography, vol. 12, University of Toronto/Université Laval, 2003–, accessed November 26, 2018, http://www.biographi.ca/en/bio/rae_john_1813_93_12E.html)

In 1844, the HBC chose Rae to lead an expedition to survey Canada's northern coastline. Travelling by canoe, dog sled and foot, from 1846 to 1854 he led numerous surveying journeys to the Arctic, covering thousands of kilometres of coast. Rae was also drawn into the searches for the lost Royal Navy expedition led by Sir John Franklin that had left England in search of a navigable passage from the Atlantic Ocean to the Pacific. Franklin had disappeared and repeated rescue attempts failed to find him.

Rae heard rumours of Franklin's ship being iced in on the Victoria Strait, pieces of wood that might be from his ship were found in Parker Bay, but there was no conclusive evidence. In

1854, moving west, he met Inuk at Pelly Bay, who had heard about a party of white men who, dragging a boat, had perished of starvation away to the west. On his return to Repulse Bay, Rae heard even more detailed accounts of the Franklin tragedy. The Inuit told him that the last survivors of the expedition had been forced to resort to cannibalism. Along the Great Fish River, they sold articles identified as belongings of the men including silverware and Franklin's Royal Hanoverian Order.

With the onset of winter, later that year Rae called off the search for Franklin's ships and returned to England, taking artefacts from the Franklin Expedition with him.

His report to the Admiralty was met with outrage. The fact that British sailors had resorted to cannibalism was unthinkable! Equally unacceptable was the testimony Rae had learned from "natives."

Franklin's widow, Lady Franklin condemned him and criticized him for lack of proof and accused him of only wanting the financial reward offered for knowledge of the Franklin Expedition. In turn, he defended the credibility of his information and explained he had received these details too late in the season to continue the search.

In 1856, Rae retired from the HBC, married and moved from Canada to England. He continued to travel, surveying for a telegraph line between Britain and America through Scotland which included journeys to the Faroes, Iceland and again to Rupert's Land, along with new territory in Saskatchewan and Alberta.

Rae died in London in 1893 and was buried in his home country, the Orkneys. His mapping of the Arctic coast of Canada was not reported in books and his discoveries were wrongly credited to Royal Navy explorers. Only recently was his name and reputation as a great explorer restored.

("Per Mare Stromness 200, 200 years as a Burgh of Barony," Stromness Museum, 2017 Exhibition. Text by Tom Muir, Foreword by Janette Park, Introduction by Bruce Wilson.)

Louie Kamookak, an Inuit oral historian and Honorary Vice President of the Royal Canadian Geographical Society grew up in Nunavut, around King William Island where the survivors of Franklin's expedition had walked to their deaths, starving and finally resorting to cannibalism after abandoning the Erebus and Terror.

Kamookak, listening to the stories of the Franklin horrors passed down orally through generations by the Elders, was convinced they could lead to the remains of the expedition ships. He combed the island, matching Inuit place names with the replacement names given by non-Inuit.

In 2014, the Erebus was found and two years later, the Terror. Both ships were found exactly where Kamookak had predicted. On March 23, 2018, Kamookak died after a self-taught career in forensic archaeology.

"The latest discovery was made two years and a day after Canadian marine archeologists found the wreck of Erebus in the same area of eastern Queen Maud Gulf, where Inuit oral history had long said a large wooden ship sank."

"....crew found the massive shipwreck, with her three masts broken but still standing, almost all hatches closed and everything stowed, in the middle of King William Island's uncharted Terror Bay."

(The Guardian, 12 September 2016)

Published in 2002, Canadian author, Ken McGoogan, wrote a detailed account of Rae's accomplishments, his rejection and discreditation by the Admiralty, Lady Franklin and Victorian society – and his vindication and return to a "rightful place in history." (Amazon review of "Fatal Passage.")

In 2017, a ceremony was held in Stromness, Orkney, granting the Freedom of Orkney to Dr. John Rae.

Since then, the John Rae Society has raised funds to purchase his ancestral home in Orphir and plans to develop it as an exhibition and conference centre. John Rae Festivals are held annually in Stromness with renowned speakers and international visitors.

THE ITALIAN CHAPEL

The exquisite church on the tiny Island of Lambholm in the Orkneys sees tens of thousands of visitors. It's a landmark that is instantly recognizable, thanks to its stark white and red façade, emerging prominently and brilliantly against the gentle green fields and sparkling waters that surround it. The chapel stands alone, fulfilling its original purpose to act as a memorial for the harsh realities of wartime and a celebration of peace.

The Royal Navy's base in the Orkneys, called Scapa Flow, is where several German ships were scuttled in 1919. To this day, occasionally you can see their wrecks poking above the surface of the water. During the Second World War, the blockage created by the wrecks, together with booms and anti-submarine nets, were expected to protect Scapa Flow from further attack.

The plan failed. In 1939, a fatal attack at exceptionally high tide allowed a German U-boat to evade the blockages and sink the battleship Royal Oak, anchored at Scapa. Over 800 sailors perished and the U-boat escaped.

Starting in 1940, the eastern entrances to Scapa were protected from attack by the Churchill Barriers. These were massive blocks of concrete placed in varying positions along either side of the barriers, at every angle and crevice, to prevent the tide from rising over the four causeways that link the islands. In 1942, Italian prisoners of war (POWs) taken during the 8th Army's North Africa Campaign began to provide the labour. 200 men were brought to Camp 60 on Lambholm.

The prisoners made paths on the island, planted flowers and one of their number, Domenico Chioccetti, an artist, built a statue of Saint George from a framework of barbed wire covered in cement. There was also a theatre and a recreation hut, but something was missing. A place of worship.

The happy combination of a sympathetic new Commandant and an Italian priest moved the project along when they organized two Nissen huts, placed end to end as housing for a chapel. There were limited materials available, so Chioccetti and his band of workers covered the ugly corrugated inner walls of the huts with plasterboard, used concrete for the altar and altar rail, and eventually added a concrete façade to the outside of the huts to resemble a church. Wood from a wrecked ship was used to build the tabernacle and the baptismal font was constructed of material from the inside of a car exhaust. Corned beef tins were even fashioned into light holders. Talk about ingenuity at its finest!

And it didn't end there. Behind the altar, reaching up to the sanctuary roof was a spectacular Madonna and Child, painted by Chioccetti, copied from a picture he carried with him throughout the war.

Candelabra in both brass and iron were made by a smith and

an electrician. Palumbi, the iron worker, built one of the other great beauties of the chapel, its rood screen and gate.

At the entrance to the Italian chapel, you'll find pictures of the men taken prisoner, along with an account of their origins in the Italian 6th Anti-Aircraft Regiment's Mantua Division and the Italian Tank Corps.

Work was completed in 1943 but the POWs had little time to enjoy their chapel. They were soon transferred to Yorkshire in September 1944, and repatriated in May 1945. The Lord Lieutenant of Orkney (and then owner of Lambholm Island), Mr. Sutherland Graeme, promised the men that the islanders would cherish the beautiful chapel they had created.

My father, Corporal Mackay, was a part of the North Africa Campaign, as he described it, "chasing Rommel all over the desert." The 8th Army continued into Sicily and Italy – a time dad spoke of with great affection for the people he came to know at the tail end of the war. We used to tease him that he must have become acquainted with a certain "Angela Maria," hence my name. But it was entirely in jest; my mother had no fears. I still have a photo of Dad at the "bathing beach café" in Genoa, on the 6th of May, 1945 – days before Victory Day and the end of the war.

Born in the working-class surroundings of Poplar, east London, Dad knew little of the Orkneys or his ancestors except the names of Thurso, Caithness and Stromness. He had no pictures or stories to give life to the words or a history to his family. The heritage from Dad was shaky largely because he'd never been there. He did know several names which became magical to my young ears, but not much more. His grandfather, a ship's carpenter, had moved to Poplar from Scotland in the 1840s. I didn't have much more than that to go on.

When I did finally pursue this part of my ancestry, I discovered that my great-great-grandfather, William Mackay, was a 'flesher' from Stromness. I knew this place and this place knew me!

Upon my discovery, my tears came as a surprise. There was a surreal connection between my origins, my father and his war experiences, Italy, and the beautiful chapel, decorated with such devotion by men so far from home, terribly lonely and in desperate need of spiritual comfort. Their devotion can be felt in every brush stroke, the intricacy of the wrought-iron sanctuary screen, the sorrowful thorn-crowned head of Christ over the entrance and the countless details perfected by prisoners using makeshift materials.

The Orkneys have a very small Roman Catholic population. Here on the Island of Lambholm that doesn't matter. Members of three different communions continue to work together on the preservation committee. In 1992, fifty years after they arrived in Orkney, eight of the former POWs returned for a visit, which included a celebration of mass, in Italian, at their chapel.

The bonds continue to thrive.

This magnificent little chapel, a place of peace and safety, continues to be cared for by the local community, visited by thousands, loved by many who may well share Chiocetti's sentiment on leaving after his last visit in 1960 when he said, "I thank…all those…for having given me the joy of seeing again the little chapel of Lambholm where, I in leaving, leave a part of my heart." ("Orkneys Italian Chapel" Chapel Preservation Committee www.orkneycommunities.co.uk/italianchapel.)

DUSHANBE, BUZKASHI AND THE RIVER OF GOLD

To Tajikistan!

I had been hired to teach human trafficking, gender and border management, and occasionally, conflict management and the training of trainers. Much of the experience was humdrum, routine and uninspiring, that is, however, for a number of "buts," whose adventures made my overall sentiment of Tajikistan anything but boring.

The first "but" was the oddness of dusty Dushanbe. In both Persian and Tajik, its name means "Monday" and it came to be known for its "Monday Market." This happened before Dushanbe became the official capital of Tajikistan, with the largest flying national flag in the world and a prized statue of King Samoil clutching what appears to be an ice-cream cone.

The second "but" was buzkashi, a traditional and intense equestrian sport popular in Central Asia. To give you a better idea, "buzkashi" translates to "goat grabbing" in Persian, which just so happens to refer directly to the game's objective.

Rival teams compete to gain control of a goat's carcass and throw it down in the goal. The opening salvos are fast, dangerous and uninhibited as each team struggles to dominate. The thrust and pull, the pounding of hoofs, the yells and screams – the whole game, if you can call it that, is quite terrifying. A rider gets hold of the carcass, throws it on the saddle and gallops off, pursued by the fastest opposing rider who leans over to grab the goat. They both pull fiercely as they ride through clouds of thickening dust. Old Russian army tank helmets are used for protection, and might I say, rightfully so!

My dominant memory of the day at the buzkashi was of choking on the dust stirred up by a thousand hooves and of being periodically terrified as the horses thundered off the main playing area in pursuit of an ever-crumbling goat carcass, heading willy-nilly towards the spectators. Let me tell you, there wasn't much space to run.

Interwoven with this was the exhilaration and excitement of those watching the horrid event and the kaleidoscope of faces, costumes, flag-waving and horn-blowing, all controlled by some unspoken kind of order that avoided complete chaos. It's a very dangerous sport for the riders and even the spectators are injured on occasion too, but it's a day out! Buzkashi represents a time to relax from the tedium of a tough existence, a chance to see friends, make some money perhaps, buy a new horse saddle or riding boots, and see the champions in action. Well, I believe it is all of these things for some spectators. For me? Not so much.

The age range of the riders came as a big surprise. Certainly, the young bloods were there, keen and vigorous, but the champs were not juniors. The oldsters had their day. These heroes were clothed in their motley assemblage of gear – many wearing old

Russian army tank helmets – riding the most splendid horses and thoroughly enjoying their fill of success and adoration.

The third "but" which pulled me from the everyday tedious experience of Tajikistan was my trip to Zarafshan – "splendour of gold."

I was invited to spend the weekend at a village in the Zarafshan Valley. It was memorable in many ways. Initially, the chaos of organization had me doubting we would ever leave Dushanbe. A Tajik colleague in the office assured me that everything would be arranged and that he would accompany us to Zarafshan. My fears were allayed. Not only did he speak excellent English, surely useful in a remote village where there were unlikely to be English-speakers, but he was a really lovely person: reliable, calm and good company. He said transport would be taken care of and I would be picked up at the hotel early the following morning.

Then came another question. Would I mind if another man, whom my colleagues thought to be a Brit, came with us? He too had been training locally. At first, I hesitated. Should I really be going into the mountains yonder with yet another unknown man!? I think it's womanly nature to think in such a way, but in truth, I knew no one intended me any harm and the trip would be an adventure. There was no need for me to be proprietary.

The next morning, transport (a dated minivan) arrived late. The driver was full of apologies. My English-speaking office colleague was nowhere to be seen. Apparently, his father had been taken into hospital overnight and he had no choice but to be with him.

Then there was another man who arrived in a funny hat. He was to be the official interpreter – as it turns out, he wasn't much of one at all.

Our travelling group now numbered five: the driver, the border guard host, two cousins, the interpreter, myself and the yet-to-be-met, unknown Brit.

It's a testament to good fortune, the benefits of Facebook, our common experience and congruent temperaments that "the Brit" (named Sami) and I remain connected to this day. As his nickname indicates, "the Brit" is part British, born of an Egyptian father and is now a Dutch citizen married to a Canadian whose parents live in Ottawa. This familiarity was comforting as we embarked on the vastness of the magnificent mountain-rimmed setting of the Asyob Valley and other northerly destinations.

The interpreter supposedly learned English in India at a military school. I doubted everything he said, partly because his English was so atrocious and partly because none of the very few words he said made any sense. Ultimately, he became a liability and we could trust nothing he translated. He was roundly told to shut up. Gestures and seriously fractured Russian, English and Tajik were fine, and we got along well enough with the other occupants of our travelling circus.

Our host, Gorinisso, sister of my student, mother of two, with an un-named and not-evident husband, had prepared a welcome feast. It was spread out on a "tapchan," the traditional furniture resembling a large bed-frame, littered with cushions for comfort, leaning, lounging, snoozing – whatever the position of choice. It was sheltered under almond and fruit trees, bursting with blossom and humming with bees. A bowl of walnuts was specifically for me! Perhaps because I was the only other woman.

It was a lazy afternoon. We happily enjoyed the leisure of the tapchan, and the bountiful peace and beauty that surrounded us. It was a perfect pause following the spectacular drive through the mountains. After the linguistic contortions of accommodating multiple languages throughout our journey, Sami and I were free to natter in English – with his occasional Dutch contribution.

When evening arrived, more food appeared, along with the local imam who sat, separate and determined, chatting with Gorinisso's husband (he remained nameless, but became increasingly friendly over time, with a crinkled, toothy grin). At first, I found the imam's appearance curious. He paid no attention to anyone other than Gorinisso's family and sporadically to one of the cousins and our driver. They chatted and ate, chatted and ate. Then, a spread of food was laid out on a smaller tapchan nearby. Occasionally, one of them snuck a look sideways, their eyes skimming our faces before returning to their chatter. The imam seemed impervious to these glances and continued munching away. He never greeted or addressed us and as dark fell, he simply faded away into the night.

I remained curious about that visit and tried to explain it to myself. To ask why he was there would have offended all manner of cultural sensitivities, and given the language challenges, likely would have been unsuccessful. The experience faded from memory for years until I worked in Afghanistan sometime later on a literacy project for the newly-formed Afghan National Police.

That was a first. I learned there had never been a "national" police force in the country. Traditionally, local policing was conducted in communities that identified trusted local men who knew local residents, and therefore were aware and suspicious of strangers. On a regular basis, "a new face in the village" would be identified as an outsider, at which point the individual would be required to prove their identity and purpose. So, these selected village men patrolled boundaries, knowing very well the terrain, potential entry points, and the risks and dangers their community faced.

Back to the Asyob Valley and it's now perfectly clear that the local imam would have been at the front of the lineup of trustworthy characters. Hence our visitor – checking us out and uncovering our purpose, intent and connection to Gorinisso's family.

We passed the test.

Gorinisso was not only generous and attentive, but she had a beautiful singing voice and came out to the tapchan the next morning to sing for Sami and I as we sat alone with an impeccable breakfast spread.

She sang Italian and Russian love songs with clarity and feeling. She had taught herself the words, none of which she understood.

Her brother and others in our "travelling circus" had a few activities in mind for the day. We were to explore the river. The Zarafshan, a tributary of the great Amu Darya, winds its way through and around both Tajikistan and Uzbekistan, where it has greater fame for the City of Samarkand, built on its banks. Remains of Neolithic habitation have been found along its course. Quintus Curtius Rufus wrote of it and its name, "spreader of gold," which originates from its gold-bearing sands.

That day, neither ancient remains nor flecks of gold were evident in the patches of muddy sludge and thick forest green waters. The river was constantly changing from sea-green streams to foam-tossed wavelets threading round black soils, scree falls and past fields brilliant with the livid colours of spring.

The glory of spring was everywhere – in the fields, pollarded plane trees lining the river bank, orchards and soaring poplars.

Donkeys, bearing riders with feet bouncing not far from the ground, trotted calmly over narrow footbridges and lone walkers trudged along stony roads beside the swift-flowing streams.

Snow on the upper mountain slopes was shrinking, its winter

beauty overtaken by the glorious awakening of spring life along the famous river.

Showing this land with evident pride, there was a troupe of cheerful guides who accompanied us, enjoying their relaxation away from the city. In the many garbled languages we shared, they told us of the history, invasions and challenges of life in this spectacular country.

On the return journey, they were quiet. As for me, I chose to continue feasting my eyes on the glorious surroundings, silently reflecting – with some humility – on the guilty pleasures of my lazy tapchan life.

LOOKING FOR ADAM

The first clue that this was going to be anything but straightforward was the moment when the tour operator announced that I would have to be accompanied on the climb, because I was "a lady alone." As a matter of fact, I was very used to travelling alone and rather enjoyed it, but he insisted to the point where I began to doubt my reading of local sensitivities. In the end, I had no choice but to agree to take a guide from Kandy to Adam's Peak.

After being cast out of Paradise, Adam reportedly first set foot on Earth at Sri Pada, the Sacred Footprint. The 2,224-metre peak is also known as Samanalakande (mountain where butterflies go to die).

All major world religions exercise a claim to the depression in a rock shaped as a footprint at the summit. It is said that Muslims believe Adam paid penance here for 1,000 years. Buddhists believe it is the footprint left by Buddha as he launched in the opposite direction toward Paradise. The Lord Shiva is also said to have settled on the peak to shed divine light.

Or does the footprint belong to Saint Thomas the Doubter, known as Didymus, the early apostle of India, who is reputed to have baptised an Indo-Parthian king at the summit?

Sri Pada is not very high but its steep sides and the many lower surrounding mountains give it the impression of exceptional loftiness. For me, the three-kilometre climb was scheduled to start soon after dark or in the early hours of the morning.

I was keen to get started, but first came the Guide.

Questionable clues soon emerged about the Guide, but trust used to spring eternal, so I bowed to local knowledge and mores and acquiesced. At first.

The time for departure was notional, to suit his convenience, so we took off late after a visit to Kandy's Botanical Gardens where I was told, "You will be here for two hours, Madam." It seemed important to make the point I would be there as long as I damn well chose. At the same time, it also felt churlish.

On departure he made emphatic claim to the best viewing spot in the front seat. His talents were not taxed, pointing out tea estates and factories as the road crawled up into the hill country. But as we passed plantations buzzing with pickers who had collection bags strapped to their heads, the game was given away. We stopped and he bought me a coconut – an excuse for him to get out and smoke since I had banned it in the car.

Upon our arrival to the designated destination, the driver stopped in a parking lot reminiscent of a grimmer sort of fairground on a public holiday. The area was cluttered with long distance buses and echoed with music blasting over loud speakers that were strung round tacky stalls selling fluorescent baseball hats and rubber gloves.

Rubber gloves?

The Guide announced I was to sleep in the car. Another clue.

This was version number four of how the night was to be spent prior to the climb in the early hours. First, he had stated that arrangements were made for me to stay in a guest house, rest, eat, sleep, leave my bags there and climb to the top – with him.

The hour for departure, from his perspective, was equally flexible – 9:30p.m., midnight, maybe 2:00a.m., after a night in the car and all my luggage left with the driver. He somehow figured I could catch both sunrise and sunset on the summit if I played my cards right – a cleverly impossible trick without camping on the summit, which was not permitted. Either he was mad or couldn't count. Or both.

It became increasingly clear that his plans emerged only as he made them up. He had no idea of where to eat, sleep or otherwise find relief from his nasty little self. His latest idea was to sit on the car for seven hours in the beastly parking lot surrounded by noise and the flotsam of a fairground overseen by a giant statue of Buddha hovering in the corner.

The face of my saviour appeared at the window.

Mr. Veerapathram of "The Green House" rescued me from the brink of disaster. The welcoming guest house, run by himself and his wife, was a few steps off the trail. There I met Werner from Munich, and Chris and Kate from Wolverhampton and sat with them chatting over a vast vegetarian supper eaten by candlelight.

The Guide and driver took off after what sounded like not very friendly talk with Mr. V. They soon came back, loud and fussy, announcing final plans. We were to sleep until 2:00a.m. and then climb together. I rather hoped he wouldn't make it. It turned out he was incapable even of not showing up.

He did in fact return, drunk as a skunk, barely able to stand, weaving and wavering into a chair by the front door.

Then the fun began. I discovered my flashlight was missing and much acrimonious argument ensued, concerning its whereabouts and who pinched it. The Guide and driver accused Mr. V, who, suitably outraged, scolded the Guide in sizzling Singala. Meanwhile, his wife grabbed me by the hand and ran me into her room where she began opening drawers, flinging boxes full of jewels onto the dresser, and tumbling silks, sandals, and an entire wardrobe of brilliant colours and sparkling lights onto the bed. She vowed that she never locked anything, so trustworthy is every worker at the guest house. Werner watched from the shadows as Chris and Kate quietly retired to sleep.

There was no respite. Accusations were bandied back and forth, while the Guide, increasingly slurred and obstreperous, demanded what time I intended to climb, how much I was paying the crook of a Mr. V, and then ordered me to leave immediately.

He tried to stand, lurched into a plant pedestal, all of which collapsed onto the floor and peered up at me churning out words I happily could not understand.

After much noise and argument, the long-suffering Mr. V threw him out and the driver dragged him off with promises to return for me in the morning. I fell into bed in a fitful sleep from midnight to 2:00a.m., continuously interrupted by water that ran all night somewhere outside the wall at the head of the bed.

We set out in the dark and cold of 2:30a.m. There was no sign of the Guide. The climb proved him unnecessary, as there was no room for deviation once launched on the trail to the top. The climb was somewhere around 4,000 steps, we were told. I lost count.

Many times, between our rather energetic strides at the beginning and the overall pained conquest of the summit, I was forced to wonder, as the heels of the person on the next step in front filled my faltering vision, what possesses otherwise rational individuals to do such a thing. The Buddhist pilgrims have their reasons, but the rest of us? Why was I, after two hours of sleep, submitting myself to such agony to see the sunrise?

The pilgrimage season begins with Poya Day in December and runs until the start of the monsoon. All that time there is a steady stream of pilgrims and tourists, their walk lit by strings of lights snaking up the mountain.

People go to see the fine view as first rays of dawn light up the holy mountain. To the west, the land slopes to Colombo and the sea. A few minutes after dawn, the sun casts a perfect shadow of the peak onto the misty clouds towards the coast. As the sun rises the eerie triangular shadow races back towards the peak, disappearing into its base.

That was why.

Mouth dry no matter how much water I sipped, lungs rasping, heart pounding and legs screaming at me to stop such foolishness, my nostrils were also assaulted by the wafting aromas of urine. Toilets along the way were rudimentary to non-existent and only for men. Thank goodness there was also the contrasting, more pleasant scent of coconut and clove oils, which were spread liberally on the hair and bodies of fellow climbing pilgrims.

There were scruffy stalls blaring out music as they sold tea, bottled water, sugary soft drinks and more sugary biscuits. Clusters of climbers rested at the stalls or on the indoor floors of crumbling concrete shelters. Maybe the earnest pilgrim gains more grace for enduring the awful conditions.

Many of the faithful were deteriorating. Some looked as if they would never make it – whimpering, frail old ladies, grey with fatigue, supported by patient youths and crying children who, refusing to go another step, also needed to be carried.

After the hours spent in numbness trying to ignore the adolescents who gaped and giggled at witticisms made at our expense, there came a huge relief upon our arrival to the guardrails that announce the last third of the climb. If no physical help, they were a psychological bonus. By this time, I was gasping for any indication of relief from the pain circulating through my body. The rails were too wide for a decent grip and were terrifyingly cold, but they gave me hope that I might make it without plunging to my death. Some comfort.

It's the coldness of these rails that feeds local superstitions of electric shocks. Hence the sale of the rubber gloves.

Halfway up I truly doubted my grip on reality, my future and all those passing profundities which are edged out of consciousness most of the time by attending to quotidian tasks.

At 5:54a.m. we arrived. Within minutes, the first light twinged in the eastern sky. We positioned ourselves strategically, ready for a dash to the western side to see the famous shadow as the sun rose. The pale lemon light spread like a growing stain, grew to yellowish-green and then deepened to a thick, dark line of deep orange etched above the jagged hills.

As if directed by a silent signal, the carpet of pilgrims stirred. Tussled heads emerged from under towels, hair was brushed, eyes rubbed and the crowd, as one, swelled around the walls. The sun was now evident, the first quarter edging above the hills, and in the numbing cold we watched, entranced, the daily wonder we had travelled such a hard journey to witness.

The hills around us slowly appeared in shades of violet to indigo, swathed like the valleys below, in wisps of blue mist. To the north was a sparkling lake of shimmering slate – molten sunshine.

The crowd breathed an orgasmic sigh as the sun rose full before us. Sigh completed, everyone rushed as one entity to the other side of the wall to watch for the shadow.

Drum and horn were played for puja and the faithful fell to prayer, interrupted by the enthusiastic ringing of a prayer bell by a group of jolly Germans who had climbed the more difficult Ratnapura route.

We watched closely for the navy blue shadow on the hills to the west, a dark pyramid formed by the Peak's shadow, thrown by the rising sun. The shadow slowly deepened in colour and form, retreating as the mountains around it fell under the spell of the rapidly rising sun.

As the final part of our mission, we climbed the few steps to view the sacred footprint.

Then the descent began. Most of the pilgrims had already left. More painful than the ascent, my calf muscles screamed in agony, knees turned to jelly and control of my limbs was out of the question as hips devised a bizarre, uncontrollable solution to staying upright and my feet went off on their own self-directed travels. A string puppet comes to mind. The descent was much further than we imagined.

There were no brownie points for me on this climb. I knew the gaping youths bore no malice but their foolishness was irksome and distracting. On even more generous reflection, I have decided the pilgrim spirit moved them and was coupled with a certain licence for being freed from the social strictures of school and parents. Perhaps an excess of pilgrim brownie points made them boisterous.

During the downward climb, as the paper wrappers, fruit skins, bottles, cans, strips of prayer flags and white cotton skeins, and the detritus of thousands of pilgrims became evident in the morning light, we determined that the whole thing was a hoax. Adam's Peak might be a gigantic mound of garbage encased in a stone façade. The distant tea estates lay before us in luxuriant crispness, while at our feet, logjams of human rubbish clogged the streams.

If my karma depends on the virtue attained by such a pilgrimage – the physical endurance, and the ability to shrug off unattractive human behaviour and the filth and grubbiness of our worldly trappings – then I should prepare for reincarnation as a cockroach. Or on second thought, perhaps a creature large enough to deal with the Guide from Hell who will doubtless return as a toad.

Close to the bottom, Werner rushed past to keep a rendezvous with the bathroom. Groaning, the rest of us laboured up more steps to the front door of the Green House and a beaming Mrs. V with her heartfelt congratulations. There was my driver waiting under a mango tree. No sign of the Guide.

In that moment, sitting in a chair was equivalent to being in paradise. Breakfast was sumptuous, delicious and leisurely. I could not stop drinking.

The journey back to Kandy in the heat of the day was Guide-free. In a display of responsibility, the driver had apparently taken him back the night before and returned to fetch me. I thanked my lucky stars.

It felt like late afternoon (not 11:00a.m.) as we weaved and I dozed through the lush estates in luxuriant bloom. Back in Kandy my body would, for days, remind me that I did it as "a lady alone." With a little help from her friends.

NO TRAINS TODAY

*I*n 2022, I travelled alone to explore further afield in the islands I already loved. I was very much looking forward to taking the ferry to various sites, both familiar and unknown. A British railways strike changed all that and instead of a leisurely wander in Orkney I returned to mainland Scotland ahead of schedule.

This was a time when planes were expensive and already heavily booked, trains were unpredictable and erratic, and long-distance buses were crowded and also heavily booked. I did, in fact, have a return ticket from Thurso-Inverness-Edinburgh, there was just one problem: no trains. This resulted in a most unusual trip – peppered with an assortment of Europeans and a surprise Canadian.

At this point, I was deep into a discovery of my own "Scottish-ness," which began a few years ago. I immediately felt at home in Orkney the first time I stepped off the ferry in Stromness in 2016.

I'm not given to mystical connections, but this was extraordinary. It felt so familiar.

This time I was travelling alone. But not for long. The initial target was the Orkney's North Ronaldsay, further north than the southern tip of Norway, followed by a return to Stromness via Westray and then back to Kirkwall and mainland Scotland. In an instant, however, the rail strike changed everything.

The first leg, from London's Kings Cross station to Inverness via Edinburgh, instead of a direct journey was sliced into three pieces. The signage came late for the travellers who were neck-craning on the concourse, followed by an ungainly, anxious gallop to the platform.

First stop: Edinburgh. Everybody off! That train decided it wasn't going any further. The promised "buses" to take passengers to their next stop proved elusive. We wandered the platforms, recognizing each other by now, looking for the train to Inverness. We found it. Except that it was forced to stop in Perth as a result of another train ahead of us which had fallen off the tracks and needed to be removed. Everybody off! This time, we moseyed into a welcoming pub at Perth station. It was quite a desolate spot, but it was the best setting to wait for the offending train to be hauled off. Red wine with friendly Malaysians. Then there came a call to hurry back – off to Inverness with two Poles from Wroclaw and a carrot-topped Scotsman. In the bizarre way of these things, it turned out the Scotsman worked for Cadbury and had just returned from a new manufacturing installation in Wroclaw.

It was perishing cold in Inverness at 11:00p.m. Alerted cabs streamed to the station. I dreaded waking Arafe at the B&B so late. Would he even open the door? The cab driver, with thoughtful care for my safety, walked me to the porch. There was Arafe, drowsy and in his pajamas. I was full of apologies as I simultaneously thanked the cab driver for the ride.

After one night's sleep in Inverness, I took a four-hour train ride north to Thurso through a grand assortment of heather-splashed hillsides, shifting skies and skittish sheep propelled by a Pavlovian scattering at the clatter of approaching trains. They were such dense animals, with muddy "arses" and disturbed eyes.

I enjoyed intermittent chatter with another Pole from Mississauga wearing a canary-coloured jacket and who was scheduled to travel on a cruise ship, docked at Invergordon. He had time to spare and asked if I would recommend Wick or Thurso for a quick visit. Turns out there was no choice. We arrived in Thurso to discover there were no cabs and no buses from station to ferry. The sign on the Thurso station door abruptly stated "Closed." The Inverness rail office promised the Travel Centre at Thurso station would help with information and planning for the ongoing journey, which was akin to an earlier promise of "in Edinburgh there will be buses."

Pyotr, the Pole, decided that, since Scrabster Port was only a 40-minute walk, he would accompany me to see a little of Thurso during his short visit. He walked halfway and then headed off with a cliff walk to explore. Scrabster was in sight and I knew it would take 45 minutes for the last leg downhill. The perennially helpful NorthLink Ferries staff explained the reality of ferry-bus schedules. They warned that on my return only the 6:30a.m. ferry from Stromness would be met on arrival by a bus going directly to Inverness. That's it. There would be no bus to meet the early ferry to take passengers to the train. The alternative would be to walk four kilometres uphill with luggage. I would have cause to remember.

I checked a lonely bus stop enroute. There were two buses per day – but not for my train or this ferry.

There was far too much testosterone in the ferry bar. It was here that I recognized the reality of being invisible later in life. I was watching the TV news, while the bar-goers obliviously stood between me and the TV without thought or glance as they proceeded to talk loudly and remove a chair from my table, banging it against mine. To them, I did not exist. I left to sit on the sundeck – much the same. Invisible again. The intermittent play of light and shadow and struggling sunshine was my entertainment until I passed "The Old Man of Hoy" when, once again, I became invisible. Passengers lined up with their phones to capture the critical moment of passing the sandstone stack.

The next morning, there was a Czech, not a Pole, at Kirkwall check-in for the quick flight to North Ronaldsay. This four-seater, generously described as a plane, was like sitting in a three-seater car with a pilot.

The wind symphony whistled, like a tuneful chorus of birds trapped in the roof.

North Ronaldsay, the most northerly tip of the Orkney archipelago, emerged slowly from frothing seas.

As we pitched and tipped towards the airstrip, I was reminded of Eddie, the pilot in Somalia, who landed on a dime in an airport bristling with weapon-filled pickups and silent, sunken-eyed men.

When we landed on the Ronaldsay strip, the rain was still pelting sideways. There was no one to meet me in spite of a request sent months back. I got a lift to the Bird Observatory from a friendly airstrip staff member. Already, disappointment was seeping into my bones.

There was little to no effort to make non-birders welcome. We were neither acknowledged nor spoken to unless the issue was forced. The woman who presumably owned the place showed me my unready room, which just so happened to be too microscopic for two dwarfs in a huddle. There were bunk beds, one folding desk chair and a small table. That's it. It also proved damply cold. The bathroom next door smelled permanently, fustily of mold, with a half-hearted warm shower that dripped constantly onto a slippery floor. No hooks for clothes or towels – only the loo seat. Beyond rustic. Was the lack of basics necessary to the experience in Scotland's most northerly switch of land? Be bold, I told myself.

I lunched alone, listening to the chatter of cheerful birder tales, really "ringers" to those in the know. Twitchers and birders were seemingly derogatory – for those who look but don't ring or record! Snobbery and exclusion abound, I was content to be unqualified.

During the afternoon there were fierce, unrelenting deluges of rain. I read until there was a pause, at which point I promptly dashed out to explore. There was relief in this wild nature after so much immobility. The wind continued blasting across the island and I revelled in the feel of it, being blown and blasted, whipped, whisked and tossed. Needles of piercing rain carried me back.

Food that night was real chicken shared in collegial closeness with the birders who invited me to their table. I tried to avoid birder-only speak and asked what everyone did when they weren't birding – a deluge followed. Glad I asked. It was such an interesting group – all male and offering much more talk of birding adventures, with at least one soulmate who shared comparable reservations about the lack of Observatory hospitality. Did the ancient Picts' comparable lack of welcome to the Norse herald their demise, but for a scattering of artifacts and the Broch of Burrian (a historical Iron Age structure)?

Apart from the birders and another singular male guest who

appeared quite ancient and very much at home reading in the round, glassed-in dining and lounge room, there was no recognition of my existence by whoever ran the place. Occasional serving staff appeared helpful but distracted. I learned later the young staff were mainly volunteers, enjoying bird discovery and wild island weather for little more than food and accommodation. That would have its attractions if the sun shone. I never learned what exactly was the research conducted by the Observatory or whether its sole contribution was the recording of migratory patterns?

The second day started out more promising, but later darkened into glowering, impenetrable clouds, not to mention the food quality deteriorated significantly. I wondered about the connection between these events.

When a chance arose, I went out. The singular road was short and straight, with little feature but the roiling surf along beaches and fields that rolled lazily away. I scouted the graveyard and a defunct mill. The interesting bits of the island – the lighthouse and the mill - were too far to attempt before the promised rain enveloped again.

The famous semi-feral, seaweed-munching sheep were a must, littering the rocky beach at the land end of a small wharf. I wondered what and how often boats docked there. The charcoal clouds were stunning, dancing around a piercing sun that shattered through them to glance off the walls of the wharf and briefly illuminate the sheltering sheep, confined by a drystone wall maintained by island residents. If there were longer intervals between the rain, perhaps a little sun and a more welcoming environment I could have enjoyed that place.

Back in the dining glass-house, the beauty of the panorama surrounded me, all shifting clouds and restless waves. And rain.

I enjoyed the company of the birders; saw no birds on land or sea; loved the dramatic seascapes and the promise of the island that weather had limited for me.

Back in Kirkwall I was awake all night and up at 4:15a.m. for the cab to the bus station for the connection to Stromness. The rain spit, the gale force wind whistled and pushed the small bus sideways along the road. Then the news: no 6:30a.m. ferry. Possibly no ferry today, but I was told to make myself comfortable in the waiting room.

Comfortable!? Yes.

There was plenty of space and an invitation by the Harbour Master to use the NorthLink Staff Room and help myself to coffee. The kindly NorthLink women at Reception endured my endless questions and offered equally endless reassurance that if the weather improved, the ferry would depart. The man who arrived, amazingly, to replenish the drink and snack dispensers, joked that his bottles contained only water. Sorry, no vodka or white wine today. At least I had a book for company.

The high winds and rain lashed at fishing boats in the harbour, bouncing them like demented dancers. The streets were awash. I had no choice but to sit tight...

Ten hours later, Deb from Vancouver arrived. We Canadians bonded immediately and spent the next few hours sharing our stories. After twelve hours of waiting, the wind dropped and we were ready to board. The blessed NorthLink staff chose Deb and I as "the most patient women" who were to board at the head of the queue. At 5:45p.m., the ferry sailed into fabulous skies and increasingly calm seas.

We docked at 6:30p.m. I had been upright for 13 hours with little preceding sleep and no food. Chocolate bars and Nescafe do not count.

We navigated through the ferry passengers and tourists until,

"Surprise!" No taxis at Scrabster and we knew the bus didn't come here but twice a day, and certainly not at his hour. Options were few. I started walking in spitting rain and hoped to flag a stray taxi. No luck. I kept walking (uphill) and accosted a man coming off duty at dockside to ask about taxis. He advised me to stop at Popeyes pub up the hill. Best advice ever. Then were was another two miles in spitting rain, luckily light on luggage.

The fine young men of Scrabster saved the day. True heroes! First, they bought me a pint and then started on the phones to search for a ride. It took a while – and a second pint – but a cab arrived and whisked me to the Weigh Inn, late, tired and hungry. I had 15 minutes before the kitchen closed at 9:00p.m. I rarely move so fast, but I made it for supper and a large red wine or two.

Did a fire alarm really sound at midnight?

My Dad so loved to say "Thurso, once Viking Thorsa, river of Thor." There was one day of rest here before the trek south began in earnest.

Walking the clifftop path arrested by the aroma of seaweed, great wide beaches full of it, I met a Slovakian who was a surf-rider, regaling me with the wonders of the surf along Scotland's north coast. He and his friends left home for Scotland from October to April and surfed what he claimed was the best in Europe. How wonderful was that? I watched them out there, dipping and plunging, riding atop the crests sweeping to shore. I envied their youth and freedom and once again bewailed the ridiculous Brexit business.

As I searched for churches (somewhat of a common theme for me) there was a young Italian, I called him Emilio, taking photos of an old, defrocked church in Thurso. His interest was in the Illuminati and their belief in knowledge of sources of energy in pre-history. They also believed that the use of decorative balls on church steeples was a way of transmitting that energy to Earth. All news to me.

He talked too of the quality of stone-cutting in churches and the ability to do it with such rare precision, whereas today buildings use pre-cast materials that require far less skill. He asked if this ability – looking at the absence of mortar in the walls he examined – and the secrecy of the skill, was a link to the trade of masons and to Freemason beliefs and practices. It all sounded credible.

Debra, the fellow Canadian, and I teamed up again for the bus ride from Thurso to Inverness and spent more time than was probably warranted discussing how to "fix" North Ronaldsay to make it an inviting and enjoyable location to visit. We decided we could make a great job of it – but the first challenge would be "to bird or not to bird," and to decide what you wanted to be and say so – with much improved marketing. It was unlikely to happen. After all, it was a bit of a stretch out there in the wild waters of the north, but fun to contemplate.

As we drove past, my eyes were caught by the Emigrants Statue overlooking the Village of Helmsdale and its harbour. It was of a woman carrying a small child on her back looking out to sea, with a boy child standing, holding her hand, looking in the opposite direction – from where they had come. Its symbolism is instant and obvious – the loss and pain of departure from the homeland along with what is known and familiar, and the movement towards the unknown, a new life with a sense of hope for what is possible.

There is a twin statue in Winnipeg and a similar statue in Epirus, northern Greece. In recognition of women's contribution to the war effort, a female figure strides forward, carrying a box of ammunition and food to the frontline fighters as Italian troops advance from Albania. She carries no children, she walks alone. Different times, different causes; similar powerful sentiment. Women alone. I have seen it.

Debra and I parted in Inverness. It was a true pleasure.

I took a nostalgic stroll on the Ness Walk from downtown Bridge Street along shores thick with trees clustering around occasional waterfalls. Heading further across the Ness Islands, I was greeted by enormous trees, centuries old. It was such a glorious respite in a busy city, rich with tranquility and beauty to refresh the spirits, and the romance of the river's journey flowing from Loch Ness to the sea.

In a town of 48,000 souls there were 10 visible churches, unlike the crumbled kirks of the rural highlands. St. Andrew's cathedral of the Highlands, on the Ness bank, classic in high Anglican style, was surprisingly appealing, beautiful and warm with its reddish stone, which was different from more common frosty grey bricks. Its rood screen was breathtaking.

The oldest church, Old High Church (St. Stephen's), reputedly held its first service in the sixth century following a visit of St. Columba who converted the Pictish King, Bruda, to Christianity. It's more famous today for the execution yard. Here, after the battle of Culloden, Jacobites imprisoned in the church were executed in the graveyard.

The Chapel Yard Cemetery, to the north of the Old High Church, with its oldest gravestone dating only from 1604, was at the site of a former Dominican priory, believed to have been established in the 13th century.

The site of the first church to offer worship in Gaelic, now enjoys its popularity as the Leakey's massive bookstore.

On my last day in Inverness, I tried haggis-flavoured chips. Only in Scotland.

After my final day of discovery, I headed out early in the morning. Thus began the saga with Theo from Romania. We met at Inverness station, which was so much more hospitable than the bus station. Theo had wandered in from travels along the west coast and as far north as Cape Wrath and Durness, in Sutherland County, the heart of Mackay territory. He asked me to watch his bags while he went to find a bank. Dark memories of advice against doing just that never occurred. There would be no improvised explosive device (IED) in this clustering of packs and bags.

An hour later he returned. We talked for hours of our travels and discoveries. I never quite understood how or why he was so footloose in Scotland, but he had travelled in the true style of one who is destined to explore and wonder.

We headed for the bus station. He would continue in Scotland as I headed south and home. On the bus I met a young woman from Latvia who loved Scotland and wanted to stay – Brexit or not – and knew people with the surname Kazaks in Latvia. Relatives of my in-law relatives?

And so, uneventfully, I arrived a day later in Heathrow to end this particular bit of exploratory travel. And guess what? I didn't miss any trains, go figure.

* * *

IN ALL MY TRAVELS, I have come to realize that one of the best parts is never knowing who you're about to meet at the next airport terminal, train stop or bird observatory. And perhaps even better, you never know what brilliantly unexpected conversations you may find yourself in as you explore those human connections that serve as a genuine grounding on this enormous and amazing home, Planet Earth.

www.ingramcontent.com/pod-product-compliance
Lightning Source LLC
Chambersburg PA
CBHW030456010526
44118CB00011B/967